Gallium Investing Outlook

Roggie Clark

Learn How To Invest in Gold Bars With This Book

Whether you're new to investing or seeking to diversify your portfolio, this beginner-friendly guide will give you the knowledge and confidence to invest in gold, and other precious metals.

https://www.amazon.com/Ultimate-Investing-Buying-Guide-Beginners-ebook/dp/B0F1KWWDXG

Learn How To Invest in Silver With This Book

Whether you're approaching retirement or already enjoying it, protecting and growing your wealth is critical. The Ultimate Silver Investing & Buying Guide For Beginners is your clear, no-nonsense guide to incorporating silver into your wealth-building strategy.

https://www.amazon.com/Ultimate-Silver-Investing-Buying-Beginners-ebook

Learn Macro and Micro Economics, With This One Book

Whether you're a student, a professional, or simply someone eager to understand the world around you, this book is your perfect introduction to the fundamentals of micro and macroeconomics.

https://www.amazon.com/Macro-Micro-Economics-Made-Beginners-ebook/dp/B0DPHTFVQG

Copyright

Title: Gallium Investing Outlook
Author: Roggie Clark

Cover Design: Roggie Clark
Editing: Renee' Clark

Printed in the United States of America

Disclaimer

The views and opinions expressed in this book are those of the author and do not necessarily reflect the official policy or position of any individual, company, or organization cited or referenced in the text.

The author is not affiliated with any of the individuals, companies, or organizations mentioned in the text, nor does the author receive any form of compensation for citing or referencing them. Some sample scenarios in this text are fictitious. Any similarity to actual persons, living or dead, is purely coincidental.

The professional information (strategies, tips, and concepts) in this text is provided on an "as is" basis, without warranties of any kind, express or implied. While every effort has been made to ensure the accuracy of the information contained herein, neither the author nor the publisher makes any representations or warranties regarding its completeness, reliability, or applicability. The information is for educational and informational purposes only and should not be interpreted as professional, legal, financial, or business advice.

This book does **not** constitute financial advice, investment guidance, or legal counsel. Any financial, business, or investment decisions made based on this book are done **at your own risk**. You should always conduct your own research and consult a **certified financial**

advisor, legal professional, or other qualified expert before making any decisions that could impact your finances, business, or legal standing.

Neither the author nor the publisher guarantees any specific results or outcomes. By reading this book, you acknowledge and agree that the author and publisher shall not be held liable for any direct, indirect, incidental, or consequential damages, financial losses, or harm arising from the use or misuse of the information contained in this text. You assume full responsibility for any actions taken based on the content of this book.

Table of Contents

- Introduction
- Chapter 1: What the Metal Is
- Chapter 2: Key Uses and Applications
- Chapter 3: Supply and Availability
- Chapter 4: How Investors May Be Positioning Themselves
- Chapter 5: What the Future Could Look Like
- Final Thoughts

Introduction

Gallium is a metal best known for its role in advanced electronics, semiconductors, and high frequency communication technologies. Even though most people never encounter pure gallium, they benefit from devices that rely on gallium based components every day, without even knowing it. Industries such as telecommunications, computing, and energy depend on gallium for materials that support efficient and high performance systems. This book gives a simple overview of why gallium is becoming more visible in discussions about emerging technology and strategic resources, and how investors can better position themselves.

Why this metal is getting attention

Gallium is gaining attention because it has become essential in producing advanced semiconductors, which power everything from smartphones to 5G networks. As the world relies more heavily on faster communication and higher data capacity, the materials behind these systems matter more than ever. Gallium based compounds, allow electronics to operate at higher speeds and greater efficiencies than many traditional silicon based components.

This shift has positioned gallium as a material that could play a major role in future technological development. Rising demand for these advanced components has naturally increased interest in gallium's role in modern electronics, so as western nations continue to decouple their supply chains, gallium mining, refining, and processing will continue to increase.

Last thoughts

This introduction highlights why gallium is becoming more visible and why understanding its role can be helpful for investors. Even though gallium remains unfamiliar to most people, it supports technologies that touch nearly every part of modern life.

Recognizing its growing importance creates a foundation for following future discussions about materials used in electronics and communication. This book aims to offer a top level overview so investors can appreciate gallium's quiet but powerful role in today's technology landscape. With this foundation in place, the next chapter explores what gallium is and what makes it unique among metals.

Chapter 1: What the metal is

Gallium is a soft, white metal that behaves differently from most elements, making it particularly interesting to scientists and engineers. It is not found in its pure form in nature but is obtained as a byproduct of refining other metals like aluminum and zinc. One of gallium's most well known features is its low melting point, which allows it to melt just above room temperature while remaining solid under everyday conditions.

Although it is not a metal people commonly see or handle, gallium has properties that make it extremely valuable in high tech environments. For instance, going back to smartphones, gallium is essential for the millions of pixels in the phone's screen. Understanding the basic identity of gallium is the first step toward understanding how it supports so many advanced technologies.

Basic identity

Gallium belongs to a group of elements known as post transition metals and is typically extracted in small quantities from larger mining operations. In its pure state, it is soft and can even melt in the warmth of a human hand, very similar to mercury, but still a trait that makes it unusual compared to most metals. Despite its softness at low temperatures, gallium is stable and remains solid in normal use, allowing it to be formed into shapes needed for industrial processes.

Again, gallium does not naturally occur as a metal but appears within the ores of other elements, primarily as a trace component. It is trapped in tiny amounts inside the ores used to produce aluminum and zinc. During aluminum processing, the ore is crushed and treated with a chemical solution that separates the aluminum material from everything else. Gallium stays dissolved in that leftover solution. From there, producers use electrical currents or special chemical reactions to pull the gallium out of the liquid.

A similar process happens during zinc refining, where gallium settles in the residue that forms during smelting and can then be separated and purified. Because gallium only shows up in small trace amounts, companies do not mine for it directly. They recover it only when they are already processing aluminum or zinc, which is why gallium supply depends entirely on how much of those metals the world is producing at any given time.

Key characteristics

One of gallium's standout characteristics is its ability to form compounds that perform exceptionally well in electronics. Gallium nitride and gallium arsenide are both used to create semiconductors that operate at high frequencies, handle high voltages, and produce less heat than many traditional materials. These compounds allow signals to move faster and more efficiently, which is why they power devices like 5G equipment, radar systems, satellite communications hardware, and high performance computer chips.

Gallium also expands slightly when it freezes, which is rare among metals and adds to its unique physical profile. This unusual behavior affects how gallium is stored and handled, since it can crack containers if it freezes and pushes outward. Despite this, its low melting point makes it useful for creating specialized alloys, heat transfer materials, and temperature sensitive components for electronics.

These traits make gallium valuable for applications where reliability, speed, and efficiency are essential. The combination of chemical versatility and practical performance helps explain why gallium has become a critical component in modern electronic systems, especially in fields that demand high power, high precision, and long term durability.

Better than silicon

What sets gallium apart from other metals like silicon, is its increasingly important role in technologies that demand high frequency performance and advanced semiconductor behavior. While most people think of silicon when they hear the word semiconductor, silicon begins to reach its physical limits in applications that require extreme speed, strong signal integrity, or stable performance under high power.

Gallium based materials step in where silicon struggles. Again, compounds like gallium nitride and gallium arsenide allow devices to switch faster, maintain cleaner signals, and operate reliably in environments where heat, interference, or electrical stress would normally degrade performance.

These advantages have positioned gallium, and its compounds as cornerstone materials for modern telecommunications, satellite systems, and next generation power electronics that must push data, energy, or signals with minimal loss. Taken together, these distinctions explain why gallium is becoming more important as technology moves past traditional limitations and into fields that require faster, cleaner, and more efficient electronic performance.

Last thoughts

Understanding what gallium is helps clarify why it receives attention in discussions about advanced technology. Its uncommon physical and chemical traits give it capabilities not found in many other metals, especially in electronics.

This foundation sets the stage for recognizing how gallium contributes to devices and systems people rely on every day. As industries continue searching for materials that support higher speeds and better performance, gallium's uniqueness becomes even more relevant. With this introduction to what gallium is, the next chapter explores how it is used and why these applications matter.

Chapter 2: Key uses and applications

Gallium will continue to play a major role in manufacturing, from semiconductors to lighting technology. As global industries continue innovating, gallium's importance has steadily increased across both consumer and industrial applications. This chapter highlights in more detail, key areas where gallium is used and why those uses matter.

Primary industrial uses

Again to recall, one of the most common uses for gallium is in electronics, and semiconductor manufacturing, as a material in transistors, integrated circuits, and high frequency antennas found in smartphones and other wireless devices. But also, gallium appears in LEDs, allowing for efficient lighting solutions that consume less energy.

Gallium based materials make it possible to create bright, energy efficient lighting solutions that last longer and perform better than older lighting technologies. Everything from modern home lighting to digital displays relies on gallium compounds to produce vivid and consistent color output. LED demand alone continues to reinforce gallium's position as a critical material in global technology supply chains.

Solar technology is another area where gallium is becoming increasingly important. Gallium based photovoltaic cells are engineered for high performance environments and are often used in satellites, space missions, and specialized commercial applications where durability and efficiency matter. These advanced solar cells outperform many traditional silicon based cells under extreme conditions, which gives them a competitive advantage in aerospace and high temperature industries. These industrial uses form the core of gallium's future demand and demonstrate its role in modern and future electronics.

Strategic or high tech uses

Gallium also plays a crucial role in high tech systems that require speed, stability, and exceptional performance. Satellite communication relies on gallium based semiconductors because they handle high frequency signals more effectively than many alternatives. Military technology uses gallium nitride in radar systems due to its ability to operate under intense power levels.

Electric transportation and power electronics benefit from gallium's efficiency, especially in devices designed to reduce energy loss and heat production. These strategic uses show how gallium supports strategic technologies that require reliable and high performance materials.

Last thoughts

Gallium's wide range of applications highlights how deeply it is woven into the technologies that shape modern life. Its presence in semiconductors, lighting, military, and communication systems reflects its critical role in advancing efficiency and performance. As industries continue to innovate, gallium's influence is likely to grow, especially in fields focused on energy, defense, and communication.

Understanding these applications helps investors understand why gallium receives increasing attention from engineers and planners. With this foundation in place, the next chapter explores where gallium comes from and how its supply shapes its role in today's technology landscape.

Chapter 3: Supply and availability

Gallium's supply and availability are shaped by the fact that it is not mined directly, but again as you recall, it is instead collected as a byproduct of refining other metals, mainly aluminum and zinc. This unique sourcing method makes gallium's production dependent on the output of larger mining industries rather than its own dedicated operations.

As demand for gallium based technologies increases, questions about long term supply, refining capacity, and global access have become more common. Right now, only a limited number of countries refine gallium in meaningful quantities, which can create opportunities for industries that depend on it to localize their supply chains. This chapter explores where gallium comes from, how much is produced, and what factors influence its availability.

Where the metal comes from

Gallium is extracted in small amounts during the refining of bauxite, the ore used to produce aluminum, and sphalerite, the main ore used to produce zinc. China has historically been the largest producer and refiner of gallium, supplying a significant portion of the global market. Other countries, including Germany, Kazakhstan, and Japan, also produce gallium, though usually at much smaller scales.

Gallium mining at scale

Global gallium production varies widely based on industrial demand and the availability of refining capacity. Again, to recall, China produces the majority of the world's refined gallium, giving it substantial influence over availability and pricing. Secondary production, which involves recycling gallium from electronic waste and manufacturing scraps, contributes a smaller but growing share of the supply.

Right now, there are no current mining operations for gallium in the United States. These production patterns and limitations highlight why gallium is often treated as a strategic material within high tech industries, and why diplomatic negotiations between the United States, and China are so ongoing and important to securing a long term supply of this rare metal.

Supply constraints or controls

Again, gallium's supply is limited by both geological and industrial factors, including the difficulty of extracting it from ore and the limited number of facilities capable of refining it. Trade policies and export restrictions can also impact availability, particularly when major producers like China adjust their supply strategies.

Environmental regulations related to refining processes may also affect production levels in certain regions particularly in the United States. Additionally, because gallium is not mined directly, again, fluctuations in aluminum or zinc industries can indirectly influence its availability. These constraints help explain why gallium supply is carefully monitored by industries and governments that rely on advanced materials for strategic, and consumer electronics.

Last thoughts

Understanding the supply and availability of gallium helps clarify why the metal is often described as strategic in modern industry. Its dependence on other mining sectors and the concentration of refining capabilities create a supply structure that differs from many other metals. These factors add complexity to long term planning for industries that depend on gallium based components.

As demand continues to rise, efforts to expand refining capacity or explore new production methods may become more important. With this context established, the next chapter explores in more detail, why gallium is becoming a more frequent topic of discussion across investment circles.

Chapter 4: How investors may be positioning themselves

As gallium becomes more important to global electronics and communication systems, early observers and investors are paying closer attention to how the metal fits into long term technological trends. Although gallium does not have a direct consumer investment market, people who follow emerging materials often analyze the broader industries and supply chains connected to it.

This high level approach focuses on understanding demand signals, production shifts, and technological growth rather than looking for buying opportunities. Because gallium supports critical components in fast growing fields, awareness matters more than speculation. This chapter outlines general ways investors may be monitoring gallium as its relevance continues to increase.

High level exposure categories

People who want to understand gallium's role in industry often follow companies involved in semiconductor manufacturing, telecommunications, and advanced electronics. These sectors rely heavily on gallium based components and tend to reveal early signs of changing demand.

Observers may also look at aluminum and zinc production trends, since gallium supply is tied to the refining of these larger metals. Additionally, industries that develop LEDs, solar technology, or radar systems often provide insight into how gallium is used and where use may expand. Tracking these connections, and possibly investing in these companies can offer indirect exposure to gallium related developments without relying on formal financial instruments.

What early adopters watch

Early adopters tend to focus on announcements involving semiconductor innovation, wafer production, new gallium nitride facilities, or updates in telecommunication infrastructure. They also pay attention to geopolitical developments, especially changes in export policies (tariffs) or strategic material planning that may affect gallium supply.

Advances in electric transportation, power electronics, and data transmission technologies can also serve as demand indicators. Some observers monitor research involving gallium based compounds to see how future technologies might incorporate the metal. These signals help form a broad understanding of how gallium's role could evolve as industries innovate.

Conceptual market awareness

Understanding gallium from a broad, conceptual perspective matters because the usual investment structures are not in place for this metal. There is no public futures market, no widely traded commodity exchange, and no straightforward way to track daily price movements.

Instead, anyone trying to understand gallium's importance must look at the industries that depend on it and the supply chain conditions that shape its availability. This means paying attention to trends such as the expansion of high frequency electronics, shifts in global manufacturing, government policies on strategic materials, and the output levels of aluminum and zinc refining, since those processes determine how much gallium enters the market.

People who study gallium tend to focus on long term developments rather than short term speculation. They watch how emerging technologies evolve, how countries plan for resource security, and how changes in industrial demand influence future supply.

Last thoughts

Understanding how people may be following gallium helps explain why the metal is gaining more attention across various industries. Investors often look at broad indicators rather than direct investment opportunities like physical metal trading, or stocks, instead focusing on trends that signal future importance.

Gallium's role in semiconductors, communication systems, and energy technologies makes it a material worth following as these sectors grow. This chapter highlights the value of high level awareness rather than specific action. With these ideas established, the next chapter explores what the future could look like for gallium as technology continues to move forward.

Chapter 5: What the future could look like

As industries push for faster data speeds, improved power systems, and more durable device components, gallium based materials are expected to play a growing role. Gallium nitride and gallium arsenide continue to show potential in areas where traditional semiconductor materials reach performance limits. At the same time, supply chain conversations and global competition have raised awareness about the need for stable access to gallium. While this book does not attempt to predict outcomes, understanding possible directions helps investors see how gallium may fit into future technological landscapes.

Potential new uses

As research continues, scientists and engineers are exploring ways gallium could support next generation computing, advanced battery systems, and quantum technologies. Gallium nitride's efficiency has already shown promise in power electronics used in electric transportation and high performance chargers. Its ability to handle high voltages and frequencies may also expand applications in robotics, automation, and high speed communication networks. Some experimental technologies are testing gallium based materials for use in medical imaging and specialized sensors. Overall, the future is bright for gallium.

Possible market expansion

Growing demand for semiconductor and communication technology may encourage more countries to develop their own gallium refining capacity rather than depend on a limited group of suppliers. Several regions are actively pursuing this shift, especially those that prioritize technological independence and secure access to strategic materials. In the United States, federal initiatives such as the CHIPS and Science Act aim to bring more semiconductor manufacturing back onshore. As part of this push, the United States is evaluating ways to secure a steady domestic supply of gallium. Building local refining capability or forming stronger partnerships with reliable allies is becoming an important part of that strategy.

Increased production of aluminum and zinc globally may also expand gallium availability. As refining technology improves, processors can recover higher percentages of gallium from the same amount of raw material, making extraction more efficient. Recycling is another area gaining attention, since discarded electronics contain traces of gallium that can be reclaimed and fed back into the supply chain. Over time, these developments could strengthen global supply stability, and make western nations less reliant on China.

Long term outlook considerations

Again, gallium's long term outlook depends on the evolution of semiconductor technology, global manufacturing priorities, and shifts in communication infrastructure. If demand for high frequency and high efficiency devices keeps rising, gallium will likely remain essential.

Efforts to reduce environmental impact may also favor gallium based systems, which tend to operate with lower energy loss. However, changes in policy, trade relationships, or alternative material development could influence how widely gallium is used. Keeping these considerations in mind helps investors understand how gallium might evolve over time.

Last thoughts

While exact outcomes are impossible to predict, the trends outlined in this chapter show why gallium remains a material worth watching. The possibilities for new applications and expanded production suggest that gallium could become even more significant in the years to come. With these ideas established, the next chapter summarizes the key points and reinforces the importance of early awareness.

Final thoughts

This book has offered a simple, top level overview of gallium and its growing importance in modern technology. From advanced semiconductors to communication systems and energy applications, gallium plays a powerful yet often unseen role in devices people rely on every day.

Each chapter explored a different part of the gallium story, helping investors understand what the metal is, how it is used, and why its relevance continues to expand. The goal throughout this book has been awareness, not instruction, allowing investors to think about gallium in a broad and accessible way. With a clearer understanding of the metal's place in technology, investors can better follow future conversations about strategic materials.

Staying informed over time

Again, staying informed about gallium means watching the industries and technologies that rely on its unique capabilities. Updates involving semiconductor innovation, 5G expansion, and power electronics can all offer clues about the metal's ongoing relevance. Supply chain developments, especially related to aluminum and zinc production, can also influence gallium availability.

Observing these broader signals gives investors a practical way to understand how gallium fits into the evolving technological landscape. With this general awareness, investors are better prepared to appreciate future conversations involving this increasingly important metal.

About the Author

Roggie "Raj" Clark is an entrepreneur and a 10-year marketing professional with a proven track record in e-commerce and digital business growth.

Having built and managed successful online stores with thousands of sales and consulted for numerous marketing clients, Roggie has mastered the intricacies of online marketing, branding, and consumer behavior. He has also written several popular books on digital marketing, SEO (search engine optimization), and programming (HTML, CSS, and JavaScript).

As a former marketing manager at a fintech company—a role he secured through his own marketing and financial expertise—Roggie gained firsthand experience in financial strategy and wealth-building.

This journey inspired him to share insights with amateur investors, helping them save money, make smarter financial decisions, and build long-term wealth. Raj currently lives in Maryland with his sister and niece.

www.ingramcontent.com/pod-product-compliance
Lightning Source LLC
LaVergne TN
LVHW022326200926
848481LV00004B/1447